STRONG
BRAVE
TRUE

STRONG
BRAVE
TRUE

GREAT SCOTS WHO CHANGED THE WORLD
- AND HOW YOU CAN TOO!

Mairi Kidd

Tom Morgan-Jones

BLACK & WHITE PUBLISHING

Do Vedą le gaol
MK
For Seumas and Ali
TM-J

Contents

Introduction

Scotland is a small, rainy country in the north of Europe where umbrellas turn inside-out and wheelie bins fly around in the wind. Scotland doesn't have a big population, but it has produced an incredible number of important scientists, writers, inventors, doctors and other thinkers, and more still have come to live and work here. Perhaps the chilly weather and long, dark winter nights keep people inside by the fire and inspire them to dream big dreams . . .

Whatever the explanation, Scotland has produced many people who have gone on to change the world. So buckle up your kilt, put down your bagpipes and get ready to come on an amazing adventure to meet some strong, brave, true Scots!

WILLIAMINA FLEMING

In 1888, Williamina Fleming recorded a cloud of gas and dust in the constellation Orion. She had discovered the Horsehead Nebula – just one of hundreds of stars and nebulae she discovered in her amazing career as an astronomer.

Williamina wasn't always a scientist. She was born in Dundee, where she worked as a teacher. She emigrated to America, but her husband abandoned her and their child. And so Williamina had to take work as a maid in the home of Professor Edward Charles Pickering, the Director of an important observatory at Harvard College.

My Scottish maid could do better!

Pickering was fed up with his young male students and instead he employed Williamina and a group of women. The story goes that Pickering told his students . . . "My Scottish maid could do better." And she did!

Williamina's most famous discovery: the Horsehead Nebula.

The Nebula – a cloud of gas and dust.

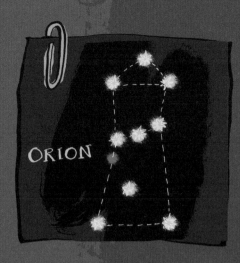

The Nebula's position within Orion.

Williamina analysed stellar spectra like these from photographs taken by Pickering's brother.

Hang on! That's not fair!

Williamina became an honorary fellow of the Royal Astronomical Society of London and received other honours, but not immediately. In fact, it took some time for her even to receive proper credit for her work. The first time her name was printed as the discoverer of the Horsehead Nebula was in 1908 – this was 20 years after she first found it.

Williamina and other women astronomers at Harvard College Observatory.

The mountains called and he went...

JOHN MUIR

The USA has 59 National Parks, which are visited by over 275 MILLION people every year. Today, these areas of wilderness are protected by law. But in the 1800s, many special places were threatened as people looked to build there, or graze their animals.

MAP Sequoia

Sequoia

MAP yes will

YOSEMITE

YOSEMITE GUIDE

GUIDE

John Muir dedicated his life to nature. He wrote about wild places and millions of people came to love and value nature when they read his books. He fought to preserve Yosemite Valley and other wild places in America, and many national parks were founded as a result of his campaigns. Lots of Americans call him 'the Father of our National Parks'.

John was born in Dunbar and lived there until he was eleven, when his family went to America. He never forgot Scotland and he visited again in 1893 – it was then that his friends noticed he hadn't lost his strong Scottish accent in over 50 years!

Today you can follow the John Muir Way from his birthplace in Dunbar to Helensburgh, 134 miles away on the West Coast.

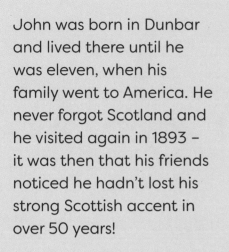

I do like a water feature! *

John built a cabin near Yosemite Falls in 1869 and lived there for two years. It had a stream running through it!

* John never said this. He did say, "I came to life in the cool wilds and crystal waters of the mountains."

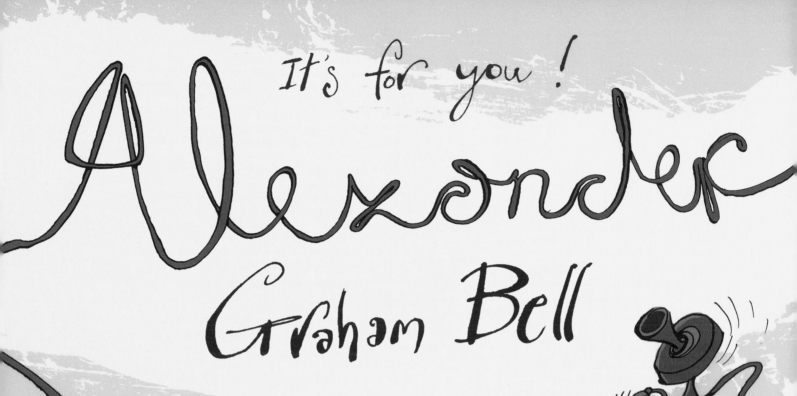

It's for you!
Alexander Graham Bell

It can take the work of many people to develop the inventions that change our lives. In the late 1800s, lots of scientists and others were working to turn speech into electronic signals that could travel long distances. Alexander Graham Bell was the first to lay claim to an invention that would let people talk to each other even when they were hundreds of miles apart.

Alexander was born in Edinburgh and had an interest in speech and hearing all his life. His mother was deaf and so was his wife, and his father and grandfather worked with people with speech and hearing problems.

Missed call? Alexander wouldn't have a telephone in his study – the sound disturbed him!

Lots of things helped develop young Alexander's interest in speech and sound.

He saw a wonderful automaton – a model that could speak!

He learned to tap out conversations so his mother would be able to join in.

Ow əh oo gə mə mə?

He taught the family dog to growl while he moved its lips and throat to make it 'speak'!

When Alexander was 23, he moved with his family to Canada. He taught deaf people in the daytime, and at night he worked on his inventions. In 1876, he made his first working telephone. He displayed it to the public and even to Queen Victoria! By 1905, there were 2.2 MILLION telephones connected to Alexander's system.

One of Alexander's deaf pupils was the famous American writer and campaigner Helen Keller. She praised him for helping people overcome 'inhuman silence' and loneliness.

What's on the box?

Another Scottish inventor, John Logie Baird, invented the television!

J. K. Rowling

When J. K. Rowling first wrote about a boy wizard called Harry, she didn't have a 'wizard' office like this one to work in.* Instead, she wrote *Harry Potter and the Philosopher's Stone* in an Edinburgh café.

She is one of many writers to have been born or lived in Scotland, and who thrill, chill or tickle us with their stories.

*J.K. Rowling's study probably doesn't look like this, but we wish it did!

Julia Donaldson

Julia Donaldson is one of the most successful authors in the world. *The Gruffalo* is perhaps her most famous creation.

Julia works with many wonderful illustrators. *The Gruffalo* is drawn by Axel Scheffler.

The Writers

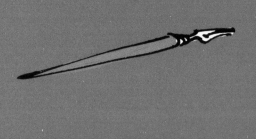

Arthur Conan Doyle

Arthur Conan Doyle's books about the detective Sherlock Holmes are famous all across the world. They have inspired many films and TV series. Elementary, my dear Watson!

Sir Walter Scott

Sir Walter Scott invented historical novels. He also made Scotland very fashionable when he arranged for King George IV to visit in 1822. His novel *Waverley* gives the main railway station in Edinburgh its name, the only station in the world named after a book!

Mary Queen of Scots

Mary is most famous as the queen who lost her head, but she was also a very talented poet. Her ancestor James I of Scotland was also a poet and writer.

J.M. Barrie

James Barrie is best known for his stories about the magical island of Neverland and Peter Pan, the boy who wouldn't grow up.

Kenneth Grahame

The author of *The Wind in the Willows* – starring 'such a clever Toad' – was born in Edinburgh and brought up near Loch Fyne.

They paved the way...

Thomas Telford

Thomas Telford built and repaired castles, churches and canals, and so many roads that he earned a new nickname. The 'Colossus of *Rhodes*' was a huge ancient statue in Greece. Telford was called the 'Colossus of Roads' instead! He also built many famous bridges and aqueducts, including the Menai Suspension Bridge, which was completed in 1826, and the Dean Bridge in Edinburgh.

John Loudon McAdam

John Loudon McAdam travelled very far in his life – all the way from Ayr to America. Perhaps his travels inspired him to develop better roads when he returned home in 1783. He began to build roads using a base of large stones, topped with a mix of smaller stones and gravel.

His roads rose a little to the middle so water could run off. 'Macadam' roads spread all over the world in the 1800s. Later, Edgar Hooley added tar to the Macadam surface, giving us the word 'Tarmac'.

John on a postage stamp in 2009.

And they cycled it!

Kirkpatrick Macmillan

Did you know that a blacksmith from Dumfries invented the pedal bicycle?

Around 1839 Kirkpatrick Macmillan got a 'hobby horse' – a contraption people pushed along the ground with their feet – and added pedals. His bicycle was very heavy, but he was fit and strong. He cycled 70 miles to Glasgow on it in 1842 – it took him two whole days!

John Boyd Dunlop

In 1887, John Boyd Dunlop watched his son struggle with his tricycle. The metal wheels were slow and heavy, and so John made new wheels from wooden discs and rubber tubes which he inflated with air. Soon inflatable tyres were all the rage. Millions of people threw away their solid bicycle tyres and fitted inflatable ones instead. Today almost every tyre on the planet is inflatable.

This is much better!

David Hume

He enlightened the world

In the 1700s, Scotland was packed with writers, doctors, engineers, scientists and other thinkers. They met to discuss their work in clubs and universities, and they wrote books and articles so that people all over the world could share in their ideas and inventions. This time is called the 'Scottish Enlightenment', because Scottish ideas were like a light that let people look at the world in new ways.

David Hume was born in Edinburgh in 1711. He went to university when he was only twelve and then he set out to spend ten whole years reading and writing. This made him rather ill, and the treatment his doctor gave him included a pint of wine every day!

David finished writing his first book when he was 28. It wasn't an instant success, but over time more and more people read it and it came to change the way they thought about human nature and the world.

In 1995 sculptor Sandy Stoddard completed a statue of David for the Royal Mile in Edinburgh. People like to rub his big toe for luck – perhaps they are hoping for enlight-toe-nment!

CHARLES RENNIE MACKINTOSH & MARGARET MACDONALD MACKINTOSH

In the early 1900s, the 'Glasgow Style' was all the rage. Buildings, furniture, clothes and lots more were decorated with patterns and designs inspired by the work of a group of young artists from Glasgow. The most famous of the artists were Charles Rennie Mackintosh and Margaret Macdonald Mackintosh. Together, Charles and Margaret designed amazing buildings. Charles drew the plans and worked with Margaret to design every detail inside, from furniture, lights and doors to fabrics and paintings.

Very few of Charles's designs for buildings were ever built, and so it was especially sad when a terrible fire swept through the Glasgow School of Art in 2015. People all over Glasgow, Scotland and the whole world love the 'Mack' as it's called, and some of the firemen were even in tears as they fought the blaze. In 2018, an even worse fire damaged the Mack further. It will be many years before the Mack can welcome students through its doors again.

AN EQUAL PARTNERSHIP

Today, Charles is better known than Margaret, but he always said he owed his success to her.

BUILDING A REPUTATION

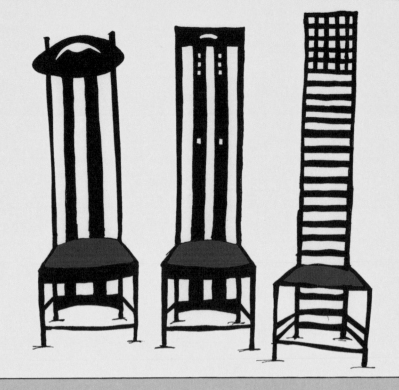

Charles Rennie Mackintosh was interested in Japanese art and loved simple lines and shapes. He designed elegant and unusual chairs and collectors pay many thousands of pounds to own them today. But although they may be very lovely to look at, they are often not so comfortable to sit on!

Margaret loved softer shapes, flowers and Celtic images. Her artwork *The White Rose and the Red Rose* was sold for £1.7 million in 2008, the most ever paid for a Scottish artwork.

MILK AND SUGAR ?

One of Charles and Margaret's main clients was Catherine Cranston, who owned a chain of tearooms in Glasgow. Margaret and Charles designed many beautiful tearooms for Miss Cranston.

DID YOU KNOW? Other famous Scottish architects include William Adam, Robert Adam and Alexander 'Greek' Thomson.

Til a' the seas gang dry...

Robert Burns

Ink

Scotland's National

BARD

Every New Year, people all across the world sing the song 'Auld Lang Syne'. It was written by Robert Burns, the son of a farmer from Ayrshire. Do you think Robert could ever have imagined that his song would become famous all over the globe?

Robert Burns was born in Alloway in 1759. His family was poor and Robert worked hard as a boy. He didn't always have enough to eat, and for the rest of his life his health was weak.

Robert's father taught him at home, and he only went to school now and then. He loved dancing and parties and his first songs were love songs. He planned to go to the West Indies but he ran out of money and so he published his poems in a book instead.

The best laid plans of mice and men . . .

In 1785, Robert wrote his famous poem 'To a Mouse'. The poem tells of how he destroyed a mouse's nest with his plough. He is sorry for the mouse's loss, and he tells her that he, too, has many worries about the future. The saying 'of mice and men' has become famous across the world.

Nae man can tether time nor tide...

Robert died when he was just 37 years old, but in his short life he wrote many famous poems and songs. Perhaps the most famous of all is 'Tam O' Shanter', the story of a man who rides home on a dark and stormy night, chased by witches. His brave horse Maggie saves the day, but she loses her own tail.

Helping to make it better...

Many Scottish doctors and scientists have changed the ways we care for the sick. Here are just three . . .

WILLIAM HUNTER studied the human body. He was born in Glasgow and worked in London, where he was the personal doctor to Queen Charlotte. People flocked to his lectures on the human body in a specially built room in his house. Later he returned to Glasgow, where you can see his collections in the Hunterian Museum.

Dem bones, dem bones . . .

William was very interested in bones and cartilage. Many of his discoveries still help doctors treat their patients today.

In the First World War an army doctor called **ALEXANDER FLEMING** saw many soldiers die when their wounds became infected with bacteria. After the war, he began to test ways of fighting bacteria. When he went on holiday in 1928, one of his samples went mouldy in his untidy lab. Alexander noticed that the mould had destroyed the bacteria. The mould was penicillin – one of the most powerful medicines in the world. Alexander won many awards, including the Nobel Prize in Medicine in 1945, so perhaps being untidy pays!

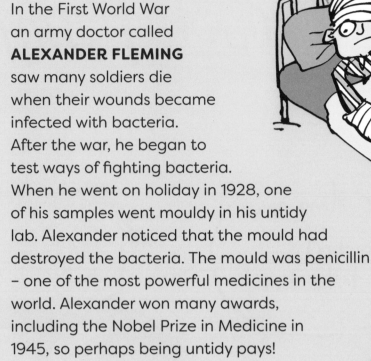

When doctor **ELSIE INGLIS** wrote to the War Office in 1914 to offer to treat wounded soldiers, she received a rude reply. But Elsie was used to battling against the odds – she had been campaigning for years for better healthcare for women, and the right to vote. The letter made Elsie even more determined. She set up her own hospitals in Europe, all run by women. They treated over 200,000 soldiers. In 2009 the Clydesdale Bank put Elsie on its £50 note to honour her work.

The Stevenson Family

This is Skerryvore Light as it looked around 1850.

They brought light to the darkness (in more ways than one)

Come along now, Robert, work to be done!

When Robert Stevenson's mother married a lighthouse engineer, young Robert soon decided to follow in his new stepfather's footsteps and started work as his assistant. By 1791 he was an expert in his own right and supervised the building of the Clyde Lighthouse on Little Cumbrae.

Robert had three sons of his own – Alan, Thomas and David. All three became lighthouse engineers. All in all, the Stevenson family built over 100 lighthouses around Scotland, an amazing feat that saved countless lives.

Robert even received a medal from the King of Norway!

Come along now, boys, work to be done!

A CHANGE IN DIRECTION – Robert Louis Stevenson

Thomas's son Robert Louis Stevenson was born in 1850 in Edinburgh. Growing up, he was often ill and he spent his time reading and writing stories. He travelled with his father to the family lighthouses, and their wild settings gave him ideas for tales filled with pirates and adventure.

Dr Jekyll is the story of a doctor who takes a potion and becomes an evil creature called Mr Hyde. Robert Louis Stevenson called it a 'fine bogey tale'.

When he grew up, Robert Louis became a writer and his classic books include *Treasure Island* and *The Strange Case of Dr Jekyll and Mr Hyde*. *Dr Jekyll* is one of the world's most famous stories and it changed the way we think about people and their personalities.

He powered great change...

JAMES WATT

YOU WATT?

Some people say that James came up with the idea of steam power as he watched a kettle boil. It's true that James used kettles in his experiments, but he did not invent steam power. He made steam engines better and more useful.

One day, 250 years ago, James Watt took a Sunday stroll that would change the world forever. James was an engineer who built and repaired all sorts of machines. As he walked across Glasgow Green, he was thinking about a kind of steam engine called a Newcomen engine, which pumped water out of mines. James was fixing a model of a Newcomen but he was unhappy with the way the system worked. Before he was halfway across the Green, James had worked out how to make the engine better. He rushed home, but he couldn't start work straight away as it was Sunday and no one in Scotland was permitted to work on a Sunday!

Full steam ahead...

Newcomen engines used steam to push a piston through a cylinder. Then water was sprayed into the cylinder to cool it down. This condensed the steam – turned it back to water – and sucked the piston back to its starting position. Then more steam was pumped in to start the process again.

James realised this was a big waste of steam, heat and coal. He added an extra chamber to the pump where the steam could turn back to water. This meant the cylinder did not have to be cooled and heated.

With this invention, James became so famous that the unit of electrical and mechanical power was named the 'watt' in his honour.

A silver lining... or a cloud?

After James made engines better, factories could produce more goods. Britain changed from a country of farmers into a place filled with factories, mills and mines. People moved to new towns and cities to find work. Life would never be the same again.

Today, we are dealing with changes made to the world by factories and power plants, chemicals and fossil fuels. Our new challenge will be even bigger than James's as we struggle to reverse the damage and protect the planet.

They mapped the world...

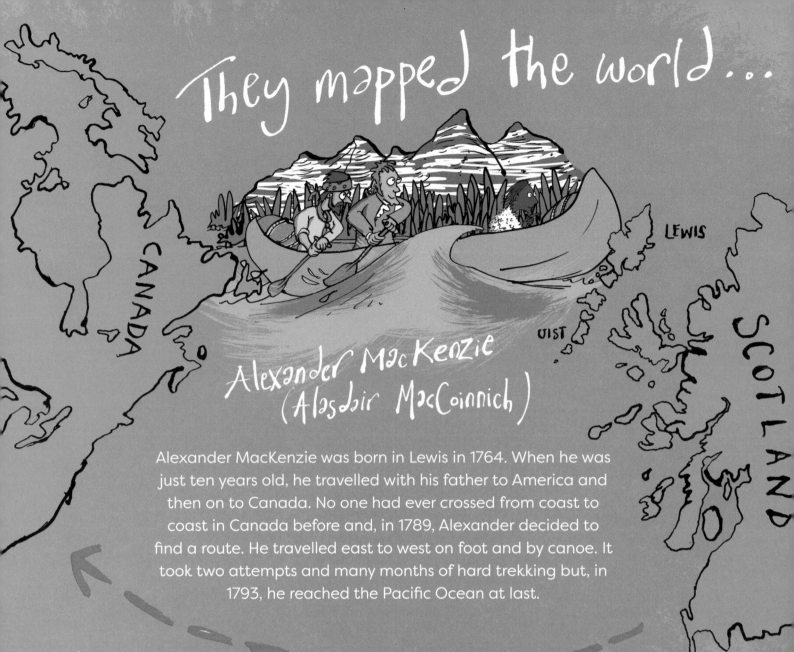

Alexander MacKenzie (Alasdair MacCoinnich)

Alexander MacKenzie was born in Lewis in 1764. When he was just ten years old, he travelled with his father to America and then on to Canada. No one had ever crossed from coast to coast in Canada before and, in 1789, Alexander decided to find a route. He travelled east to west on foot and by canoe. It took two attempts and many months of hard trekking but, in 1793, he reached the Pacific Ocean at last.

John Rae

In 1845 there were still big blanks on maps of Canada. The explorer Sir John Franklin had vanished trying to find a sea route through the Arctic to the Pacific Ocean. John Rae, a doctor from Orkney, was part of a search party sent to look for Franklin. John had many friends among the local Inuit people. He wore Inuit clothes, preferred igloos to tents and was so good at walking in snowshoes that he had the nickname Aglooka – 'he who takes long strides'. A group of Inuit told him where Franklin had died, and how to find him. John didn't get proper credit for his own discoveries – perhaps because he was not rich like Franklin and because people in Britain looked down on his Inuit friends.

I do like this wild sort of life!

Isobel Wylie Hutchison

In 1939 a reporter from *The Scotsman* newspaper visited Isobel Wylie Hutchison at her home near Edinburgh. He wrote,

Miss Hutchison is, you feel, much too fragile and gentle for Arctic exploration.

He was very wrong about Isobel! She loved to walk and she dreamed of travelling to far-off lands. First she began to walk across Scotland, and then she walked from Reykjavik in the south of Iceland to Akureyri in the north. She wanted to visit Greenland next and, to get permission, she had to offer to study the plants that grew there.

Golly! I will have lots to tell if I ever get home again!

Isobel took two long trips to Greenland between 1927 and 1929. After Greenland, Isobel travelled to Alaska where she survived long months trapped by ice. She even boarded a 'ghost ship' sailing along on an ice floe! She took some notepaper from the ship to write home.

Woof!

Other famous Scottish explorers include David Livingston, Mungo Park and Alexander Gordon Laing. What can you find out about them?

Isobel collected hundreds of plant specimens, painted hundreds of pictures and wrote books and poems about her adventures in some of the remotest places on the planet. She won the Mungo Park Medal for her work as an explorer.

Wha's like us?

Violet Jacob

A.L. Kennedy

Edwin Morgan

Carol Ann Duffy

Iain Crichton Smith
Iain Mac a' Ghobhainn

Norman McCaig

Robert Fergusson

Jackie Kay

Liz Lochhead

Sorley Maclean
Somhairle MacIlleathain

Edwin Muir

Hamish Henderson

Muriel Spark

Hugh MacDiarmid

Just a few of Scotland's amazing writers, past and present

Dr Who has been Scottish twice!

James McAvoy

Ewan McGregor

Peter Capaldi

David Tennant

Sean Connery

Actors who brought characters from James Bond to Jedi to life

26

Historical heroes

Robert Bruce

William Wallace
(as played by
Mel Gibson)

Flora MacDonald

Risked or gave up their own lives to help others doing church work overseas

Mary Slessor   Jane Haining

Helped set up the Bank of England

William Paterson

Màiri Mhòr nan Òran

Gaelic poet and land campaigner

Craig Furguson   Billy Connolly

Stan Laurel

Made the world laugh

Invented waterproof fabric and gave raincoats the name 'macs'

Charles Macintosh

Alasdair Gray

John Byrne

Allan Ramsay

Eduardo Paolozzi

Henry Raeburn

Just some of Scotland's amazing artists

Legendary trainer of warriors

Sgàthach

Founder of the Labour Party

James Keir Hardy

Chefs and a marmalade maker!

Tom Kitchin

Tony Singh

Janet Keiller

John Witherspoon

James Wilson

Signed American Declaration of Independence

John Murray

Published many of the most famous writers of all time

They named an Oxford college after me

Mary Somerville

Astronomer and mathematician

Merida

Groundskeeper Willie

Oor Wullie

Shrek

Made up but still Scottish!

29

The greatest Scot of all?

It doesn't matter if you were born in Scotland or moved here or came for a visit – you can be strong, brave and true too. And it goes without saying that no one has to be Scottish to be great! What might YOU do to change the world?

Anyone can do great things. Believe in yourself, and believe in other people. Don't give up when the going gets tough, and stand up for the things you believe in. Be inspiring, and be inspired. Ask questions, find out answers and discover new things. Everyone has talent and ability – find out what you are good at and what you care about, follow your dreams and don't be afraid to take chances . . .

You can

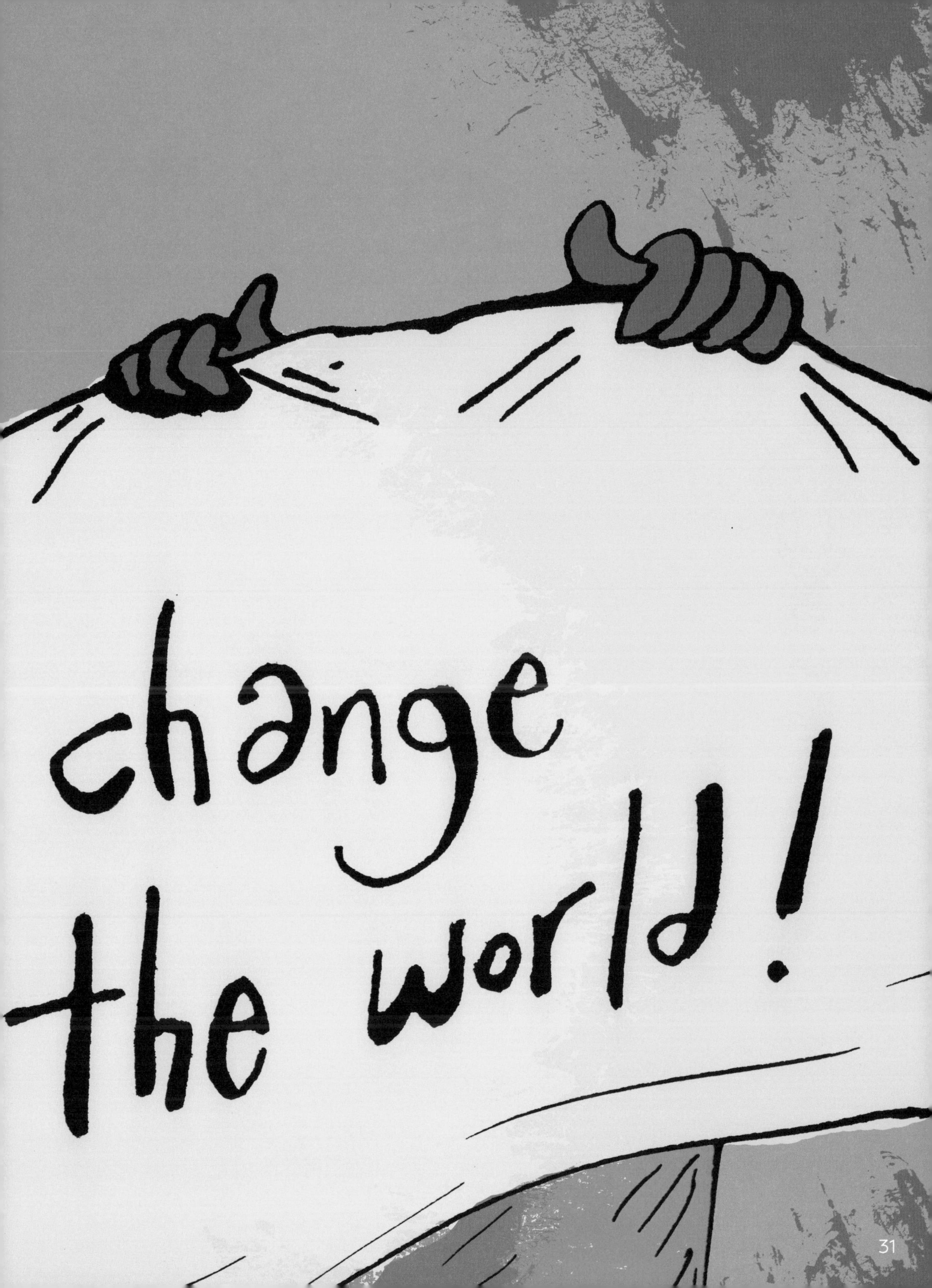
change
the world!

Taking Great Care

A note for grown-ups and enquiring young minds

You may notice there are more men than women in this book. Throughout history, men have had more chances than women to make their way in the world. This is changing and in the future we should see many more great Scottish women make a name for themselves. This fact also makes the achievements of Williamina, Margaret, Elsie and our other strong, brave and true Scottish women even more impressive.

Many of the people in this book lived hundreds of years ago. Their ideas made a huge difference at the time, but in some cases our understanding has changed. We may now see that their methods were not quite as they should have been. For example, Alexander Graham Bell disliked sign language. He wanted to find ways to 'cure' deafness and to reduce the number of people born deaf. Many deaf people do not accept that they should be 'cured'. They believe that Alexander was wrong, and that deaf culture including sign language has an important place in the world.

It is also important to understand that when our Great Scots went to places like Canada, there were already people there. These people were generally not treated well by European settlers. The new settlers often did not respect them or their knowledge, so when we say that a European 'discovered' a particular place or route, we should remember that the people already living there had quite possibly known about it for generations. Our Great Scots benefitted from local guides' knowledge. John Rae was unusual for his time in the level of respect he had for Inuit people.

Some of the European explorers in other countries were missionaries – they took their Christian faith to the places they visited. They went with good intentions, but many people think that it was wrong of them to wish to introduce their faith and lifestyles in place of the faiths and lifestyles of people in these countries.

As we told you, many people may work together to develop an invention or idea, and different people may come up with the same invention or idea separately but around the same time. Sometimes there are fights over who created an invention. The person who registers the invention may have the best claim, or they may have the most money and the best lawyers. Some people say that Alexander Graham Bell is not the real inventor of the telephone, and John Boyd Dunlop may have invented his tyre on his own, but someone else had already registered the idea of inflatable tyres. It is a complicated area and often comes down to decisions made by law.

On the other hand, some of the strong, brave and true Scots in the book did more than we have told you. Alexander Graham Bell also helped invent the metal detector and audiotape, for example!

First published 2019
by Black & White Publishing Ltd
Nautical House, 104 Commercial Street, Edinburgh, EH6 6NF

1 3 5 7 9 10 8 6 4 2   19 20 21 22

ISBN: 978 1 78530 251 0

Layout by www.creativelink.tv
Printed and bound by Opolgraf, Poland